CD INCLUDED

TODAY'S PIANO GREATS

A STEP-BY-STEP BREAKDOWN OF 13 H...

T0082004

BY TODD LOWRY

HAL•LEONARD®
CORPORATION

7777 W. BLUEMOUND RD. P.O. BOX 13819 MILWAUKEE, WI 53213

ISBN 978-1-4768-1420-9

Printed in the U.S.A.

First Edition

Visit Hal Leonard Online at
www.halleonard.com

CONTENTS

INTRODUCTION

This book/CD is a guide to various piano styles and techniques used by the giants of today's pop and rock music. The artists and songs encompass a wide variety of styles ranging from the driving rock of "Clocks," to the mellow acoustic pop of "Don't Know Why," to the gentle balladry of "How to Save a Life," to the goth rock of "My Immortal," to the jazz-infused "Ordinary People." What the diverse artists all have in common is that the songs are piano-driven.

The musical selections in this book are basically pop tunes and the piano parts serve their overall effect. Therefore, most of the examples consist of comping patterns. "Comping" is musicians' lingo for "accompaniment." A comping pattern is a rhythmic and harmonic background for the vocal melody. Sometimes these comping patterns are very basic, perhaps consisting of simple, sustained block chords or repeated triads. Other times, the piano part is technically more challenging. A wide variety of comping styles is found herein, including block chords, repeated chords, broken chords, rolling chord patterns, octave unisons, and left-hand octave patterns. Also, most of the songs have introductions and/or instrumental interludes that showcase the piano.

A study of the piano styles herein reveals a rich harmonic vocabulary, frequently incorporating chord inversions, extended chords, slash chords, add9 chords, pedal tones, and unique and daring chord progressions. The music is certain to be enjoyed for generations to come. We hope this book/CD will contribute to the appreciation and understanding of it.

THE RECORDING

Follow the audio track icons in the book to find your spot on the demo CD. The icons are placed after the figure numbers at the top of each musical example. Timings shown in the printed music refer to the original artist's recording.

CLOCKS

Words and Music by Guy Berryman,
Jon Buckland, William Champion
and Chris Martin

From the Coldplay album
A Rush of Blood to the Head (2002)

"Clocks" is from British rock band Coldplay's second album, *A Rush of Blood to the Head.*

Written by all members of the band, "Clocks" won Record of the Year at the 2004 Grammy Awards and it reached No. 29 on the Billboard Hot 100 chart. It is probably the song most associated with the band. The song is built around a hypnotic piano riff that may be the band's signature creation.

The music for "Clocks" is written with four flats, but it is actually in the mode of E-flat Mixolydian, with all the Ds flatted.

"Clocks" is a great example of using an economy of musical ideas for maximum dramatic effect. The musical materials basically consist of three simple, three-note broken triads. The triads in this case are E♭ in first inversion, B♭m in second inversion, and Fm in root position. The E♭ triad is played for four beats, the B♭m for eight beats, and the Fm for four beats. The notes of each triad are played in eighth notes in the order of top note, middle note, bottom note, top, middle, bottom, top, and middle. This forms a rhythmic pattern of 3+3+2 eighth notes. The band plays this in a driving rock fashion with accents on beats one, the "and" of two, and beat four.

Figure 1 – Intro
The song begins with Coldplay keyboardist Chris Martin playing the four-bar piano riff twice with both hands in octaves over a synth pad. The band joins in for two more repetitions accenting the 3+3+2 rhythm. The same four-bar riff is later played beneath the Chorus.

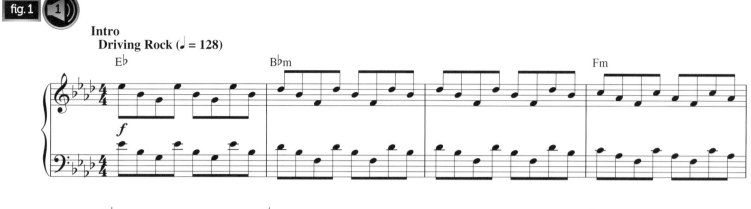

Figure 2 – Coda

The Coda begins with the band dropping out and the solo piano playing the four-bar riff two times over a synth pad. Then, at bar 5, the band joins in again while the piano plays a new figure in the right hand over the familiar chord progression in the left hand. The rhythm in the right hand is still in groups of 3+3+2 eighth notes.

The Chorus is sung over this new figure. Then a new vocal part is introduced featuring the words, "Home, home, where I wanted to go." The riff continues to be repeated and eventually the band fades out.

Coda 3:25

Chorus

You _____   are. ___

Home,   home, ___   where I want - ed ___ to   go.

Play 4 times

Repeat and Fade

DON'T KNOW WHY

Words and Music by Jesse Harris

From the Norah Jones album
Come Away With Me (2002)

"Don't Know Why" was the second single from Norah Jones's 2002 breakthrough album *Come Away With Me*. Although the song peaked at only No. 30 on the Billboard Hot 100 charts, it went on to win three Grammy Awards in 2003 – for Record of the Year, Song of the Year, and Best Female Pop Vocal Performance.

"Don't Know Why" is a wistful, mid-tempo pop ballad about regret. The instrumentation is piano, acoustic guitar, acoustic bass, and percussion.

The piano part is quite understated. Pianist Jones lets the guitar and bass do most of the harmonic work while she adds background colors and fills. One technique she uses prominently in the song is both hands playing unison either in octaves or two octaves apart.

Figure 3 – Second Verse and Chorus

In the second Verse, Jones plays unison lines with both hands two octaves apart. Bar 2 features a chromatic line outlining the chord movement. Bars 4 and 5 feature a five-note pentatonic fill.

Note: The B♭ pentatonic scale is B♭, C, D, F, and G.

Jones includes grace notes in her fills. A grace note is a quick ornamental tone played directly before a main note. The two (or more) notes are connected with a small slur marking. Grace notes are sometimes called "crushed notes" and we also sometimes refer to the use of a grace note on a piano as "bending a note," because it sounds similar to a guitar player bending a string. Obviously, each note on the piano is a discrete pitch, so we can't actually bend a note like a guitar player can by pulling on the strings. Therefore, we use grace notes on the piano as the closest approximation to literal bending.

Here's how to perform grace notes: If the grace note is a black key and the main note is one half step higher or lower, you can try playing the black key and quickly sliding the same finger off the black key onto the white key. If both the grace note and the main note are white keys, play the grace note with one finger and the main note with the next finger in very quick succession.

At the Chorus, Jones plays broken chords in bars 9 and 10 and a syncopated fill over F7 in bars 11 and 12. More broken chords are used in bars 13 and 14 and a figure in octaves in bars 15 and 16 basically doubles the descending bass line and vocal melody. The lick on beat four of bar 16 is a standard country piano lick featuring a "turn." The F is played with the fifth finger, while the lower notes are played with fingers 2, 3, 2, and 1.

Figure 4 – Piano Solo

The piano solo is played over the chord changes of the verse. It begins with both hands in unison two octaves apart and ends with the hands in unison one octave apart. The notes are primarily in the B♭ pentatonic scale. The solo also makes generous use of grace notes.

In bar 1, the piano merely outlines a B♭ chord. In bar 2, it gets rhythmically active with syncopated punches. Bar 4 contains the same country riff as used in Figure 3. Bar 6 contains double chromatic grace notes in both hands, further creating the illusion of bending notes on the piano.

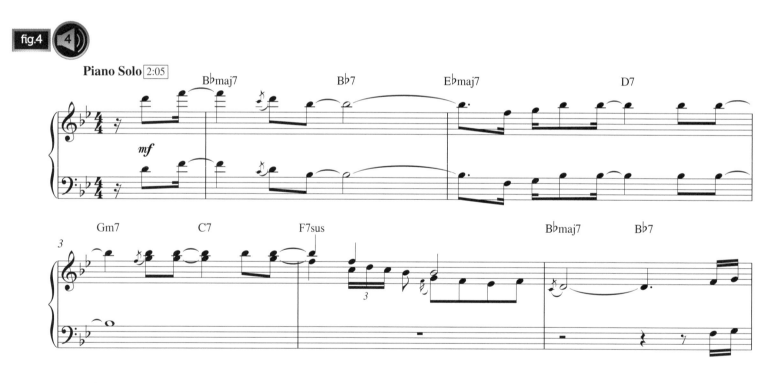

HOW TO SAVE A LIFE

Words and Music by Joseph King
and Isaac Slade

From The Fray's album
How To Save a Life (2006)

"How to Save a Life" is the title track of the debut album by the American rock band The Fray. The single was released in 2006 and peaked at No. 3 on the Billboard Hot 100 chart.

According to lead singer, pianist, and co-writer Issac Slade, the song was influenced by his experience working as a mentor at a camp for troubled teens. It is about reaching out to those who are troubled. The singer laments that he was unable to save a friend because he did not know how.

Figure 5 – Intro, Verse, and Chorus
The poignant, tender ballad begins with a lilting piano intro that suggests child-like innocence in its simplicity. The left hand, playing in the middle range of the piano, plays a bass note with the pinky finger and a broken-chord pattern with the thumb and third finger. The broken chord is gently syncopated, emphasizing the "and" of beat two.

Note: The eighth notes of the broken chord can be played by either the right hand or the left hand, but I think it's easier to play with the left hand, so that's the way it's presented here.

The pattern alternates between a B♭ chord in root position and an F6 chord in first inversion. This chord is written as F6/A and is known as a "slash chord." A slash chord is a chord with a note other than the root in the bass. Slash chords spice up chord progressions and make the bass line more interesting. As the left hand plays the chord pattern, the right hand plays a simple melody in whole notes about an octave higher.

The two-chord pattern continues beneath the vocal melody in the Verse.

At the Chorus the chords change and the right hand plays block chords, four beats to a chord, with a moving melody in quarter notes at the top of the chord. The left hand holds octave bass notes.

fig. 5

Intro, Verse and Chorus
Moderately ($\quarternote$ = 118)

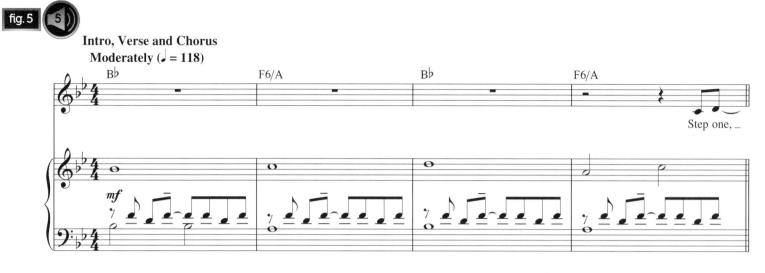

Step one, __

Verse 0:11

__ you say __ we need ____ to talk. __ He walks, __ you say, __ "Sit down,

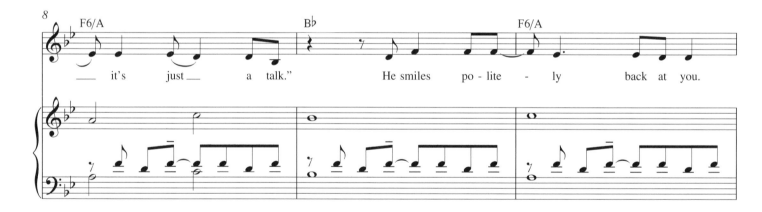

__ it's just __ a talk." He smiles po - lite - ly back at you.

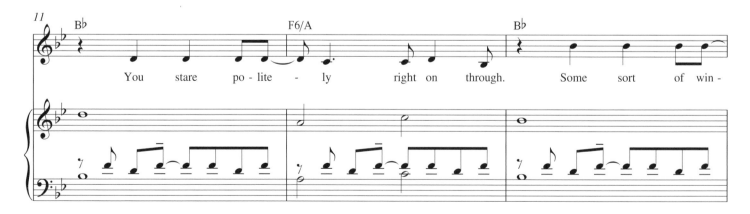

You stare po - lite - ly right on through. Some sort of win -

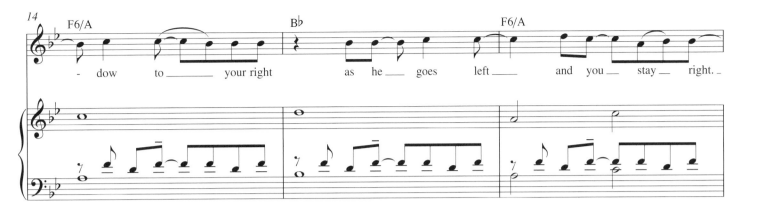

Chorus [0:42]

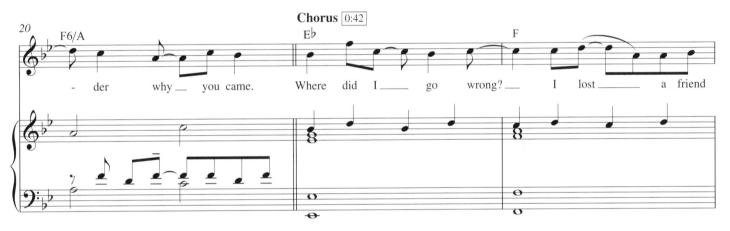

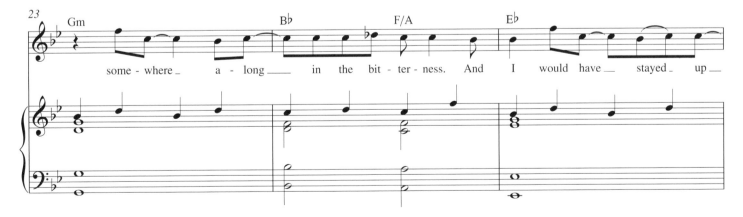

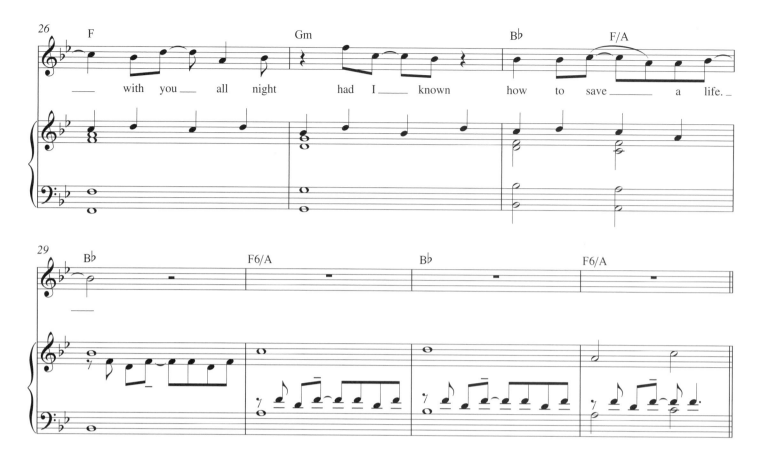

Figure 6 – Coda

In the Coda, the piano figure from the Intro is reiterated with the addition of a simple quarter-note melody in the right hand in bars 5–8.

fig. 6

How   to   save ____ a   life. ____

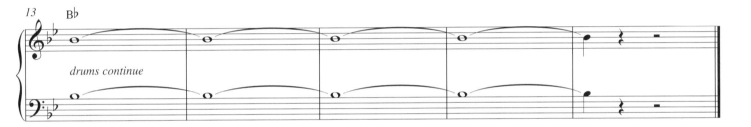

drums continue

JAR OF HEARTS

Words and Music by Barrett Yeretsian,
Christina Perri and Drew Lawrence

From the Christina Perri album
lovestrong (2010)

"Jar of Hearts" was the debut single by American singer-songwriter Christina Perri. It peaked at No. 17 on the Billboard Hot 100 charts. "Jar of Hearts" has been described as an autobiographical song by Perri, recalling an ex-boyfriend who wanted to rekindle their broken romance. The instrumentation of the song consists solely of vocal, piano, and some expressive strings.

Figure 7 – Verse and Chorus

There's no Intro. The song begins with the piano playing whole-note block chords in the mid-range of the piano under the vocal melody. Pianist Perri plays a broken-chord fill in bar 4 and a passing chord of E♭/G in bar 8.

At bar 9, the right hand begins to play block chords in a quarter note rhythm while the left hand plays bass notes in a half-note rhythm. The right-hand chords are all in the baritone range of the piano. The quarter-note block chords are also used in the Chorus. A minor IV chord is utilized to good effect in bars 4, 9, and 11.

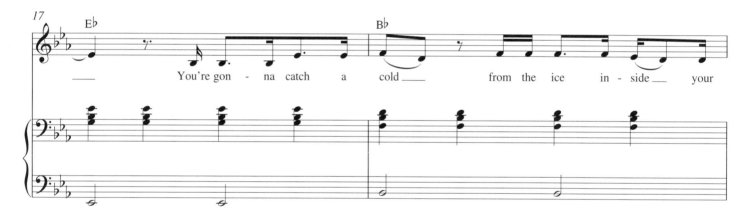

Figure 8 – Second Chorus and Bridge

In the second Chorus, the piano plays rolling chords in an eighth note rhythm, while the left hand plays a bass note every two beats.

At the Bridge, both hands shift registers, with the right hand now playing in the soprano register and the left hand revolving around middle C. Both hands play broken-chord patterns in a constant eighth-note rhythm. At bar 14 both hands shift down an octave, but continue the broken-chord eighth-note pattern.

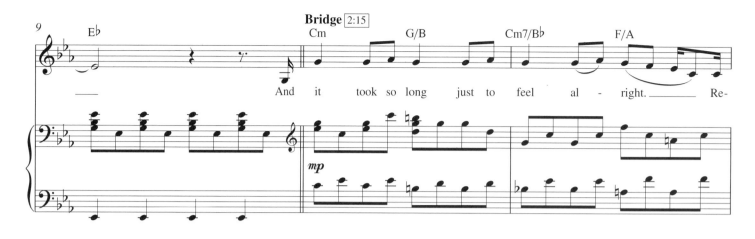

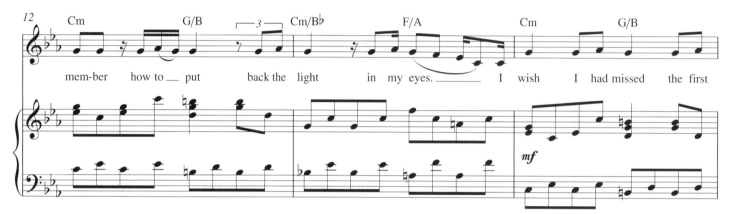

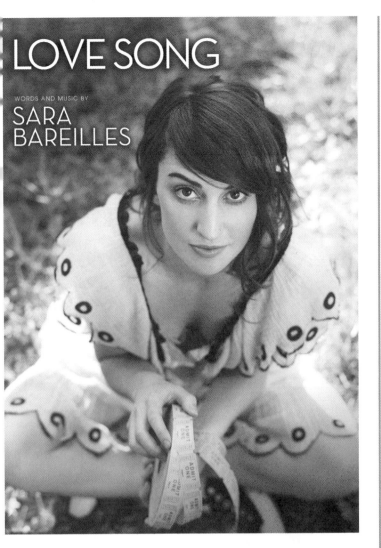

LOVE SONG

Words and Music by Sara Bareilles

From Sara Bareilles's album
Little Voice (2007)

"Love Song" was singer-songwriter Sara Bareilles's debut single, released in 2007. It peaked at No. 4 on the Billboard Hot 100 chart and it remained on the Hot 100 chart for 54 weeks.

The song is set to an irresistible, bouncy shuffle beat.

Figure 9 – Intro, Verse, and Chorus

Notice the marking after the tempo indication at the beginning. This means that all the eighth notes are to be played as "swing eighths." That is, the second of each pair of eighth notes is played on the last *third* of the beat, rather than on the midpoint between beats. This rhythmic feel is commonly known as "swing" or as a "shuffle." The shuffle feel is partly what gives "Love Song" its infectious quality.

In the Intro, pianist Bareilles establishes the main riff of the song – a four-bar chord progression with an ascending bass line. Bareilles plays three-note, close-position triads in the right hand on each beat, including a B♭sus2 chord (B♭, C, and F). These triads are played short and clipped. Meanwhile, the left hand plays a bass line in octaves that ascends the scale from G to F. This line is syncopated against the straight four of the right hand with accents on the "and" of three and the "and" of four.

The four-bar piano Intro is repeated four times verbatim as the harmonic basis for the Verse. In the second part of the Verse, starting at bar 21, the triads on every beat continue in the right hand and the chords change every four beats. The left hand switches to a bass pattern in octaves that accents beats one and the "and" of beat three.

The right hand continues its triads on each beat in the Chorus. The left hand continues its octave pattern while the bass guitar walks the bass line. After the Chorus, the Intro reappears as an interlude before the second verse.

Figure 10 – Bridge

The Bridge starts in D minor, the relative minor of F major. The right hand still plays triads on every beat, but now in a higher register.

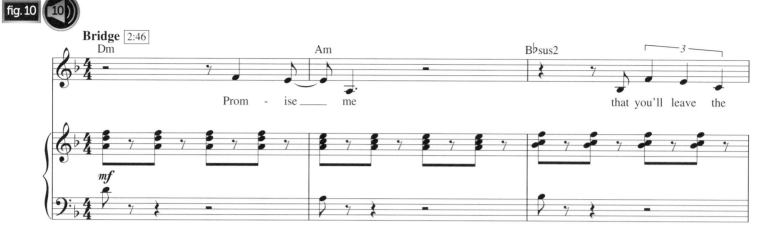

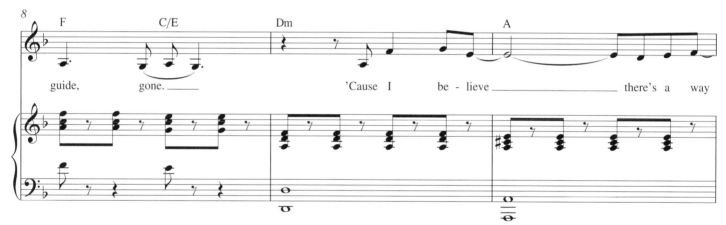

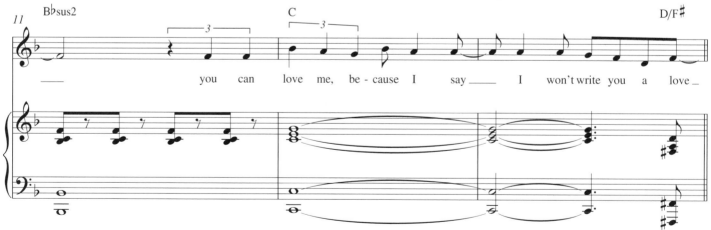

MY IMMORTAL

Words and Music by Ben Moody,
Amy Lee, and David Hodges

From the Evanescence album
Fallen (2003)

"My Immortal" was the third single from the debut album of the American gothic rock band Evanescence. "My Immortal" peaked at No. 7 on the Billboard Hot 100 charts. The band received a 2005 Grammy nomination for the song.

The lyrics refer to a spirit that haunts the memory of a grieving loved one and the song is an appropriately haunting and slow ballad.

Note: There are several recorded versions of "My Immortal." The comments here are based on the official video version of the song, filmed in black and white, which features the full band entering forcefully near the end of the Bridge.

Figure 11 – Intro, Verse, and Chorus

In the Intro, pianist Amy Lee plays a quiet, broken-chord figure in eighth notes on the chords A–C#m–A–C#m in the right hand, while she plays the root, fifth, and octave of each chord with the left. In the second A chord (bar 3), she plays a B in the right hand as a passing note instead of the chord note C#.

This alternation of the chords A and C#m continues under the vocal melody of the Verse for eight bars. At bar 13, the chord shifts to F#m (the relative minor of A major) and the music becomes stormier with broken chords in 16th-note rhythms in both hands. Bar 14 features successive intervals of a sixth in the right hand.

The Chorus features a two-bar chord pattern. The first bar starts on F#m, moves to an accent of E/D on the "and" of 2, and then it resolves to D major on the "and" of 3. This is followed by a bar of E major and C#m.

This two-bar chord progression is played eight times in the Chorus. The right hand uses a variety of broken-chord figures and some fills in scale-motion (such as in bars 18 and 20). The Chorus comes to a climax with the right-hand figure in bar 24, which leads to the low octave E in the left hand. Then it's back to the quiet Intro figure.

fig. 11   11

Intro
Slowly (♩ = 68)

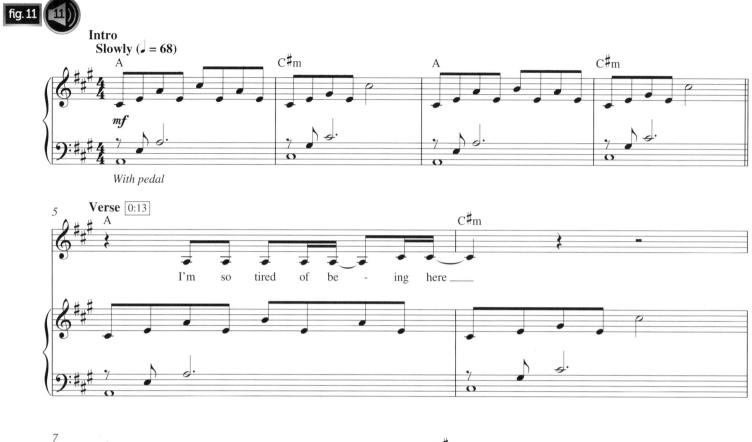

With pedal

Verse 0:13

I'm so tired of be - ing here _____

sup - pressed by all ___ my   child - ish fears. _____

And if you have to leave _   I wish that you would just ___ leave.

'Cause your pres-ence still lin - gers here ___ and it won't leave ___ me a - lone. ___

These wounds won't seem to heal. ___ This pain is just too

Chorus 0:51

real. There's just too much that time can - not ___ e - rase. When you cried, ___ I'd

wipe a - way all ___ of your tears. ___ When you'd scream, ___ I'd fight a - way all ___ of your fears. ___

Figure 12 – Bridge

The right hand gets intense in the Bridge with syncopated 16th-note rhythms moving at times in scale motion and at times in broken-chord patterns.

Triads in the right hand are heavily accented in bars 5 and 6. Bar 7 features the note G♯ temporarily suspended over a D triad before the G♯ resolves to F♯.

The full band enters in bar 9 on the accented chord progression F♯m–D–E–C♯m. The right hand plays fills in bars 10 and 11.

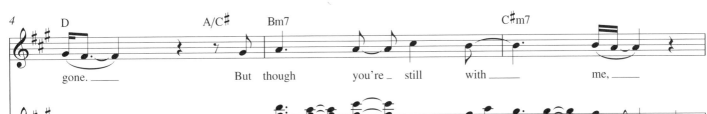

32

NO ONE

Words and Music by Alicia Keys,
Kerry Brothers, Jr. and George Harry

From the Alicia Keys album
As I Am (2007)

"No One" is from R&B singer-songwriter Alicia Keys' third studio album, *As I Am*. It is Keys' biggest hit, having topped the Billboard Hot 100 charts for five consecutive weeks in 2007. The song also won Best Female R&B Vocal Performance and Best R&B Song at the 2008 Grammy Awards.

The song is piano-driven, using the simplest of resources: the piano part consists of a single-note melody line played only by the right hand.

Figure 13 – Intro, Verse, and Chorus
The Intro begins with piano and percussion. Pianist Keys plays broken chords in eighth notes in the middle range of the piano. A four-bar chord pattern consisting of E, B6, C#m7, and A forms the basis of the Intro, Verse, and Chorus.

After the four-bar Intro, the Verse begins with the vocal. At bar 13, a fat synth bass line is added.

The piano plays the Intro pattern verbatim three times under the Verse. At bar 17, the notes of the pattern change slightly, but the harmonies remain the same. At the end of the Chorus, the pattern reverts to its original form.

Figure 14 – Coda

The Coda features vocal "ohs" over the same chord pattern of E, B, C♯m, and A. The piano plays the pattern three times.

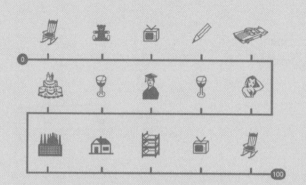

100 Years

Recorded by FIVE for FIGHTING on Sony Records

Words and Music by John Ondrasik

EMI MUSIC PUBLISHING

EXCLUSIVELY DISTRIBUTED BY
HAL•LEONARD® CORPORATION
7777 W. BLUEMOUND RD. P.O. BOX 13819 MILWAUKEE, WI 53213

100 YEARS

Words and Music by John Ondrasik

From the Five for Fighting album
The Battle for Everything (2003)

Five for Fighting is the stage name of American singer-songwriter John Ondrasik. "Five for fighting" is an expression used in ice hockey when a player receives a five-minute penalty for fighting. "100 Years" was the first single from the Five for Fighting album *The Battle for Everything*. The song reached No. 1 on the Billboard Hot Adult Contemporary chart and No. 28 on the Billboard Hot 100 chart.

In "100 Years," the singer looks back at various moments in his life and concludes that time passes too quickly. What's important is to live in the moment and recognize that "every day's a new day."

Figure 15 – Intro, Verse, and Chorus

Ondrasik's solo piano intro immediately establishes the nostalgic mood of the song. The leaping G octaves create a feeling of expectation and the chords Ondrasik uses (such as the C and Am7 chords, which lack thirds) sound open and free. The left hand plays the bass notes in a gently syncopated pattern in the middle range of the piano.

Melodically, the Verse is essentially a reiteration of the eight-bar Intro played two times.

At the Chorus, the piano changes to a fuller style with the left hand now playing in the bass register. The right hand plays syncopated figures and broken-chord patterns.

At bar 31, the chords are rich and full: Em7, D(add4), and C (add 9), with octaves in the left hand.

After the Chorus, beginning at bar 35, there's a four-bar piano interlude featuring a G/B chord moving to a Csus2 chord and later a Gmaj7/B moving to a C(add9) chord. The chord voicings in this section are rich and colorful. The "voicing" of a chord is essentially the chord shape. It includes the way the notes of the chord are arranged vertically, how they are spaced, whether any notes of the chord are doubled, and whether the chord is in root position or an inversion. Chord voicings are an expressive device in their own right.

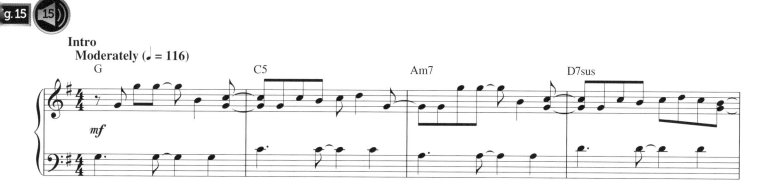

Intro
Moderately (♩ = 116)

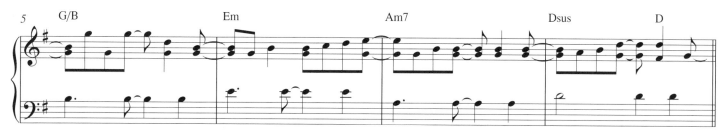

Verse 0:16

I'm fif - teen _____ for a mo - ment, caught in ___ be - tween _ ten and twen-ty, and I'm _

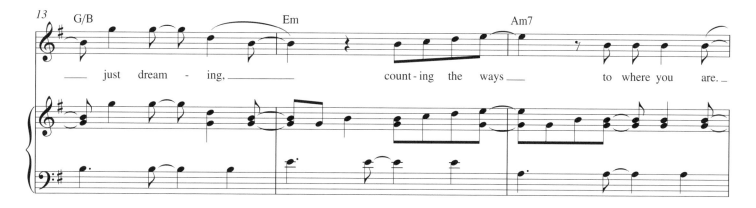

____ just dream - ing, _____ count-ing the ways ____ to where you are. _

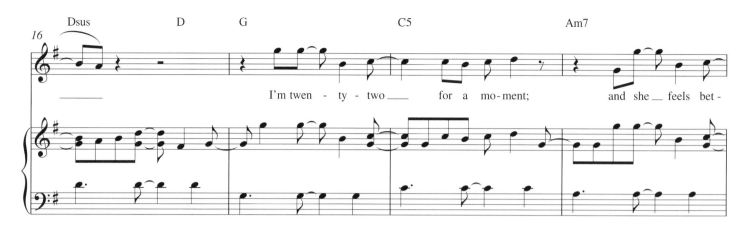

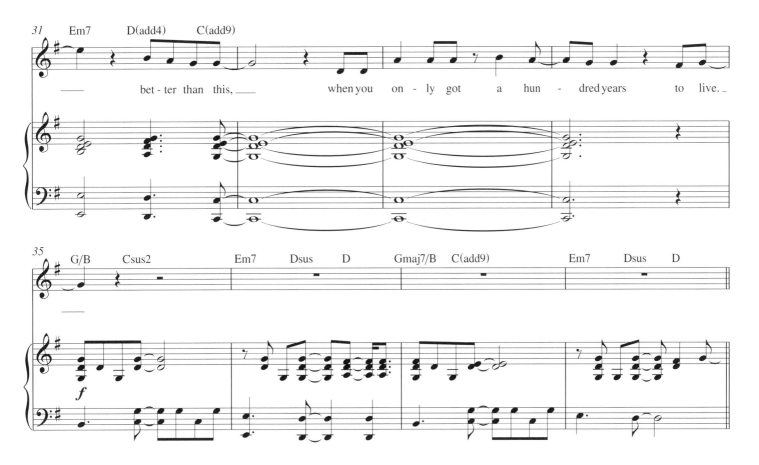

Figure 16 – Coda

The Coda features vocal "oo's" over further vibrant chord voicings in the piano. For instance, note the G with no third in bar 1 and the Csus2 chord in bar 8.

The "oo's" are followed by a reprise of the Chorus, with slightly different chords than before.

The last four bars are a reprise of the Intro. In the last bar the music slows and the song ends unresolved on a D7sus chord.

Ordinary People

RECORDED BY
JOHN LEGEND

Words and Music by John Stephens and Will Adams

SPECIAL SONGWRITERS HALL OF FAME EDITION

ORDINARY PEOPLE

Words and Music by John Stephens
and Will Adams

From the John Legend album
Get Lifted (2005)

"Ordinary People" was the second single from John Legend's album *Get Lifted*. The song peaked at No. 24 on the Billboard Hot 100 chart and won the Grammy Award for Best Male R&B Vocal Performance.

The exquisite ballad documents the difficulty of romantic relationships, as Legend sings, "We're just ordinary people/We don't know which way to go/'Cause we're ordinary people/Maybe we should take it slow."

Legend's beautiful vocal is accompanied only by piano. (In the official video version, a string section and harmonica are added near the end.)

Figure 17 – Intro, Verse, and Chorus
The music is written with two flats, but it is actually in the key of F major.

Legend makes great use of major seventh chords. In fact, the Intro, Verse, and Chorus are all built on a series of three major seventh chords: B♭maj7, E♭maj7, and Fmaj7. The B♭maj7 is played for one bar, the E♭maj7 for two bars, and the Fmaj7 for one bar.

A major seventh chord is a major triad that also contains a seventh that is a major seventh above the root. Major seventh chords have been commonly used in all kinds of popular music for generations. However, usually the major seventh chord is built on either the tonic (I) or the subdominant (IV) of the scale. Here, the E♭maj7 chord is based on the flatted VII of the scale and it leads to the tonic Fmaj7. Basically, the E♭maj7 chord is used as a substitute for the dominant chord. This unusual chord progression works to great effect.

Legend uses arpeggiated chords prominently in the right hand. An arpeggiated chord is one in which the notes are not played at exactly the same time but are played in quick succession. Arpeggiated chords (also known as "rolled chords") are written with a squiggly vertical line in front of the chord. The chord is played quickly from the lowest note to the highest note, giving the chord a harp-like effect, or perhaps emulating a guitar player strumming a chord from lowest note to highest.

Note: Occasionally, arpeggiated chords are played from top to bottom. This is shown by adding an arrow to the squiggly line pointing down.

The Intro begins with a melodic foreshadowing of the "take it slow" lines of the Chorus. The right hand is gently syncopated and plays the arpeggiated chords in triads, while sometimes adding the octaves. The left hand has its own syncopated rhythm, usually playing the root, fifth, and octave of the chord.

The piano part is played "dryly" with little or no pedal. Legend emphasizes some of the left hand notes, making them short and pointed.

Legend uses various kinds of fills: scale-like patterns (bar 6), broken chords (bar 37), and octaves (bar 13).

Figure 18 – Coda

The Coda contains more variations on the major seventh chords, such as the broken chords in bars 5 and 14. When Legend goes into his high falsetto at bar 9, the piano follows suit, playing a broken chord in the high register.

A *molto rallentando* on E♭maj7 in the penultimate bar leads to the final chord on F. Here, Legend employs a kind of stock ending common in jazz, which I call the "pretty tones ending." That is to say, Legend dresses up the final F chord with "pretty tones," including the major seventh, the sixth and the ninth of the key, making the last chord an Fmaj13. After Legend strikes the F octave in the left hand, the right hand plays chord tones in quick succession, rising to the high register of the piano.

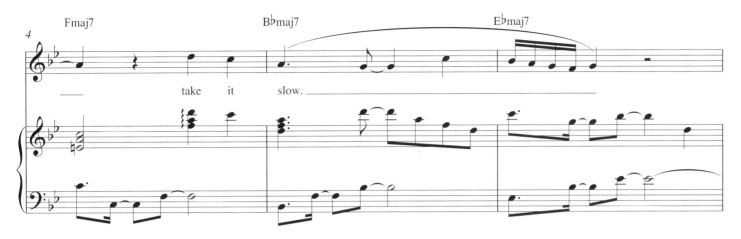

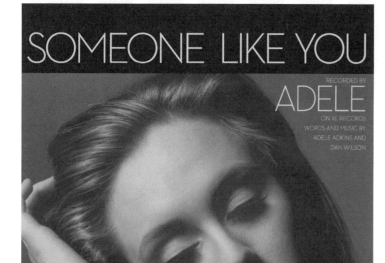

SOMEONE LIKE YOU

Words and Music by Adele Adkins
and Dan Wilson

From the Adele album
21 (2011)

"Someone Like You" was co-written by British singer-songwriter Adele Adkins and songwriter-producer Dan Wilson. It appears on Adele's second album, *21*, released in 2011.

This haunting, heart-wrenching ballad was inspired by a broken relationship of Adele's. In a vocal of aching beauty with desperately sad lyrics, she comes to terms with the end of the relationship: "Sometimes it lasts in love, but sometimes it hurts instead."

The song topped the Billboard Hot 100 chart in the U.S in 2011 and won the 2012 Grammy Award for Best Pop Solo Performance.

Like "Ordinary People," "Someone Like You" is a rarity in contemporary pop music – a song consisting solely of vocal and piano accompaniment, with no other instrumentation. The sparse, bare-bones approach serves the introspective nature of the song well. The sensitive piano on the recording was played by co-writer Wilson.

The song has a slow tempo of 60 beats per minute, although it is sometimes performed even slower by Adele in concert.

Figure 19 – Intro, Verse, and Chorus

The piano introduction immediately establishes the main piano motive: a right hand broken-chord pattern in smooth, constant 16th-notes with a broken triad on each beat. The piano plays this pattern steadily throughout the song, seldom straying from the constant 16th-note rhythm.

The right hand begins in the middle range of the piano with an A major triad in root position (with the finger pattern 1-3-5-3), followed by C#m in second inversion, F#5 in root position, and D in second inversion. The chords change every four beats with the left hand playing intervals of either a fifth or a sixth in whole notes.

The initial four-bar chord pattern is played once in the Intro and is played three times in the Verse.

Starting at measure 17, there's a five-bar transition into the Chorus. The chords now change more frequently and include a colorful E(add9) chord.

The Chorus is built on a four-chord pattern of A–E–F#m–D5 with two beats on each chord. The right hand continues to play 16th-note broken chords, though the chord voicings are opened up a bit, usually covering an octave. The left hand plays half-note bass notes either in octaves or fifths.

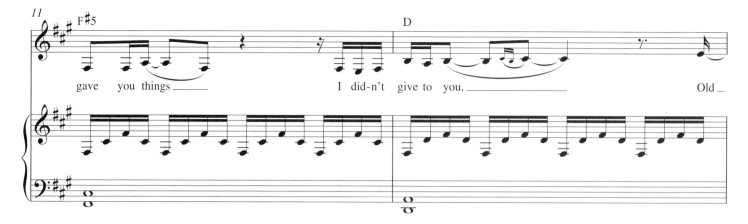

gave   you things _____   I   did-n't   give to   you. _____   Old ___

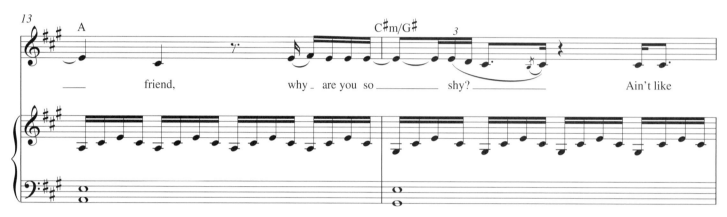

_____   friend,   why _ are you so _____   shy? _____   Ain't like

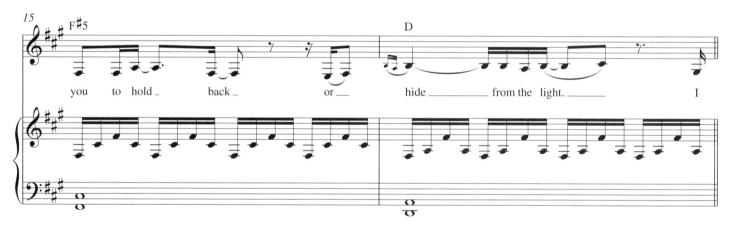

you   to   hold _   back _   or _   hide _____   from the   light. _____   I

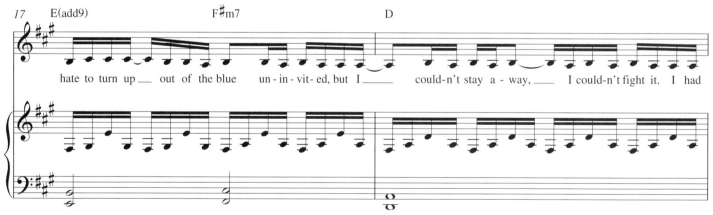

hate to turn up __   out of the blue   un-in-vit-ed, but   I _____   could-n't stay a - way, ___   I could-n't fight it.   I had

mem-ber _____ you _ said, ___ "Some-times it lasts in love, but some-times it hurts in-

- stead." _____ Some-times it lasts in love, but some-times _ it hurts _ in-

- stead, _____ yeah.

Figure 20 – Bridge and Chorus

In the five-bar Bridge, Adele double-tracks her vocals with some spine-tingling harmonies. The constant 16th-note broken chords continue in the right hand, but with new chord forms, including E/B and F#m/C#.

In the last two bars of the Bridge (bars 4 and 5), the piano gets softer and in the last bar of the Bridge (bar 5) the piano *ritards* in a wistful manner before it launches into another Chorus.

At the Chorus, the constant 16th-note rhythm of the piano finally changes as the piano plays block chords in a half-note rhythm. At measure 10, the right hand shifts to a rolling eighth-note pattern as it alternates between intervals of either a fifth or a sixth.

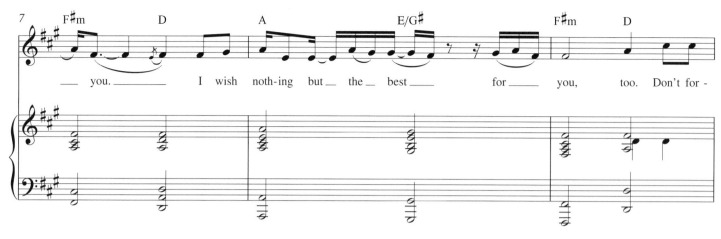

you. ____ I wish noth-ing but __ the __ best ____ for ____ you, too. Don't for -

get me, I beg, ____ I ____ re - mem-ber ____ you __ said, ____ "Some-times it

lasts in love, but sometimes it hurts __ in - stead." _____

SOMEWHERE ONLY WE KNOW

Words and Music by Tim Rice-Oxley,
Richard Hughes and Tom Chaplin

From the Keane album
Hopes and Fears (2004)

"Somewhere Only We Know" was the first single from English rock band Keane's debut album *Hopes and Fears*. It peaked at the 50 spot on the Billboard Hot 100 chart.

Keane has been known as the "band with no guitars" because of its piano-based sound. On some recordings Keane uses delay and distortion effects on the piano, but on "Somewhere Only We Know" the sound is powerful, crisp, and clean.

Figure 21 – Intro, Verse, and Chorus

The piano style here is a more refined, second cousin of Jerry Lee Lewis. That is, triads in the right hand are pounded out in a propulsive rhythm of eighth notes while the left hand plays bass notes in octaves.

Pianist Rice-Oxley employs a technique where he plays a chord several times and then changes one note to alter the quality of the chord and plays that chord several times. For instance, in bar 2 he plays A5 three times, then Asus three times, then A two times, all over a G# bass note. In bar 4, he plays Esus three times, then E three times, then Esus twice. This technique tends to keep the harmonies shifting somewhat ambiguously.

After the eight-bar Intro, the Verse is accompanied by only the right hand of the piano playing close-position triads in a repeated eighth-note rhythm.

The Chorus shifts from A major to the relative minor, F# minor. The right hand continues to play repeated close-position triads and the left hand plays bass notes in octaves.

Figure 22 – Bridge

Rice-Oxley expands his right-hand voicings in the Bridge, usually covering an octave. He also employs more four-note chords and even a five-note chord in bar 7. The right-hand eighth-note rhythm continues unabated, while the left hand plays octave bass notes.

A THOUSAND MILES

Words and Music by
Vanessa Carlton

From the Vanessa Carlton album
Be Not Nobody (2002)

"A Thousand Miles" was the first single from American singer-songwriter Vanessa Carlton's debut album *Be Not Nobody* (2002). The song reached No. 5 on the Billboard Hot 100 charts and remained on the charts for 41 weeks. It was nominated for three Grammy Awards.

The song is in the unusual key of B major. When you play in unfamiliar keys, you are less likely to produce stock clichés and this song definitely is not about clichés.

While the lyrical situation is fairly stock – the singer pines for her missing lover – the harmonies are appealing, the melody catchy, the string arrangement dramatic, and the piano lines fresh. The song is sort of like a mini-musical in its own right.

Figure 23 – Intro, Verse, and Chorus

Pianist Carlton opens the song with one of the most audacious piano hooks in pop history – a quasi-classical swirl of leaping octaves and propulsive 16th notes by the right hand in the high register of the piano, with quickly shifting harmonies suggested by the left.

After the four-bar piano Intro, the Verse features a two-bar vocal phrase that is then answered by the Intro figure, now played an octave lower. Again, there's a two-bar vocal phrase answered by a reiteration of the Intro figure.

At bar 13, the piano plays three simple chords answered by the vocal. This happens three times. While these piano triads are overshadowed by the heavy strings, check out the voicing of the B(add9)/D♯ chord: D♯, B, C♯. The great American rock band Steely Dan had a name for this chord voicing. They called it the "Mu" chord.

In the Chorus, the piano plays a three-note syncopated motive (A♯-B-F♯) in the right hand with octave bass notes in the left. The Chorus resolves on a dominant F♯ chord in bar 24, and again the Intro hook is played, this time with the right hand playing in the high register and the left hand playing octaves in the bass register.

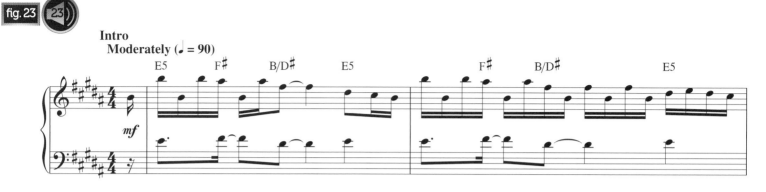

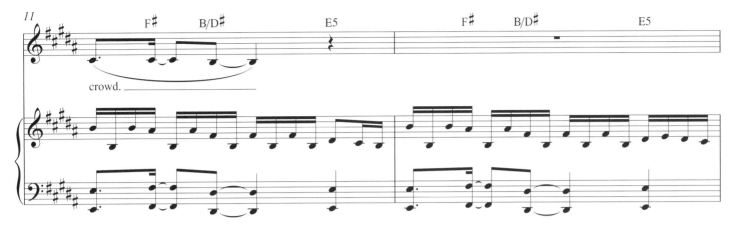

Figure 24 – Coda

The Coda begins with a reiteration of the Chorus. Again, we have a three-note motive (A♯-B-F♯) repeating in the right hand over octaves outlining a chord progression in the left. The chords under the lines "if I could just see you"

in bars 7 and 8 are repeated an octave higher in bars 9 and 10. Finally, the introduction is reiterated with the piano ending on an unresolved E6 chord, with no third.

fig. 24   24))

you think___ time___ would pass me___ by?___ 'Cause

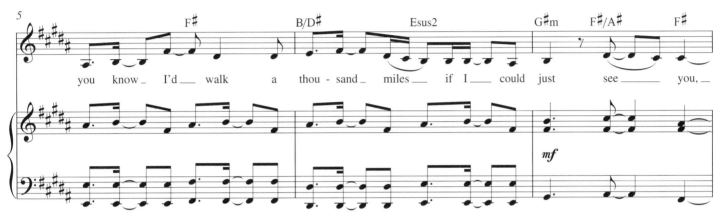

you know___ I'd___ walk a thou-sand___ miles___ if I___ could just see_____ you,___

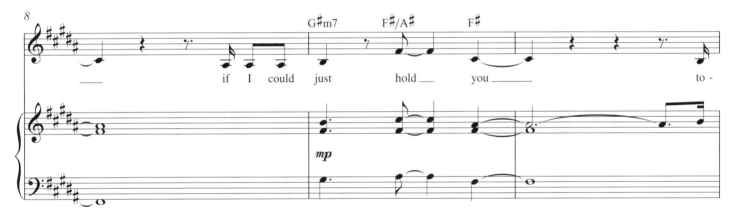

___ if I could just hold___ you_____ to -

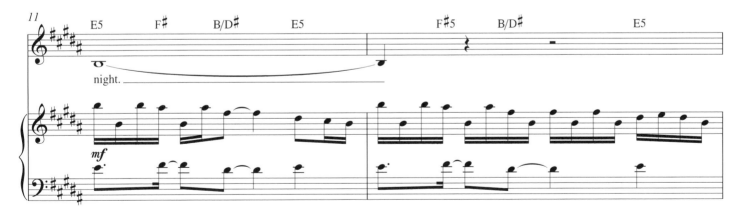

night.___

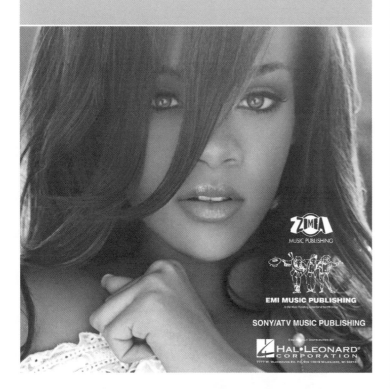

UNFAITHFUL

Words and Music by Mikkel Eriksen,
Tor Erik Hermansen and Shaffer Smith

From the Rihanna album
A Girl Like Me (2006)

"Unfaithful" was recorded by Rihanna on her second studio album, *A Girl Like Me*. The R&B ballad is dark and moody and is sung by a woman who regrets cheating on her partner. The song peaked at No. 6 on the Billboard Hot 100 chart.

"Unfaithful" is in the key of C minor and features a prominent piano part, a dramatic string arrangement, and percussion.

Figure 25 – Intro, Verse, and Chorus

The song begins with a four-bar piano intro featuring an insistent, syncopated riff in the right hand revolving around the notes C, D, E♭, and F, moving in scalar motion over chords emphasizing the minor key.

This four-bar piano Intro, repeated twice an octave lower, serves as the accompaniment for the first eight bars of the vocal melody.

At bar 13, the right hand of the piano basically doubles the vocal melody, while the left hand plays the bass root, fifth, and octave of each chord.

In the Chorus, the piano riff becomes even more insistent, emphasizing the notes C, D, and E♭ over changing chords. After the Chorus, the piano Intro is repeated.

Figure 26 – Bridge

The Bridge continues with the emphasis on the notes C, D, and E♭, moving up a step with each successive chord change. At measure 5, there is a new variation of the piano riff, featuring leaping octaves in the left hand.

THE ULTIMATE SONGBOOKS

HAL·LEONARD
Piano Play-Along

These great songbook/CD packs come with our standard arrangements for piano and voice with guitar chord frames plus a CD.

The CD includes a full performance of each song, as well as a second track without the piano part so you can play "lead" with the band!

2. JAZZ BALLADS
00311073 P/V/G..............$14.95

3. TIMELESS POP
00311074 P/V/G..............$14.99

4. BROADWAY CLASSICS
00311075 P/V/G..............$14.95

5. DISNEY
00311076 P/V/G..............$14.95

6. COUNTRY STANDARDS
00311077 P/V/G..............$14.99

7. LOVE SONGS
00311078 P/V/G..............$14.95

8. CLASSICAL THEMES
00311079 PIANO SOLO..............$14.95

9. CHILDREN'S SONGS
0311080 P/V/G..............$14.95

10. WEDDING CLASSICS
00311081 Piano Solo..............$14.95

11. WEDDING FAVORITES
00311097 P/V/G..............$14.95

12. CHRISTMAS FAVORITES
00311137 P/V/G..............$15.95

13. YULETIDE FAVORITES
00311138 P/V/G..............$14.95

14. POP BALLADS
00311145 P/V/G..............$14.95

15. FAVORITE STANDARDS
00311146 P/V/G..............$14.95

17. MOVIE FAVORITES
00311148 P/V/G..............$14.95

18. JAZZ STANDARDS
00311149 P/V/G..............$14.95

19. CONTEMPORARY HITS
00311162 P/V/G..............$14.95

20. R&B BALLADS
00311163 P/V/G..............$14.95

21. BIG BAND
00311164 P/V/G..............$14.95

22. ROCK CLASSICS
00311165 P/V/G..............$14.95

23. WORSHIP CLASSICS
00311166 P/V/G..............$14.95

24. LES MISÉRABLES
00311169 P/V/G..............$14.95

25. THE SOUND OF MUSIC
00311175 P/V/G..............$15.99

26. ANDREW LLOYD WEBBER FAVORITES
00311178 P/V/G..............$14.95

27. ANDREW LLOYD WEBBER GREATS
00311179 P/V/G..............$14.95

28. LENNON & MCCARTNEY
00311180 P/V/G..............$14.95

29. THE BEACH BOYS
00311181 P/V/G..............$14.95

30. ELTON JOHN
00311182 P/V/G..............$14.95

31. CARPENTERS
00311183 P/V/G..............$14.95

32. BACHARACH & DAVID
00311218 P/V/G..............$14.95

33. PEANUTS™
00311227 P/V/G..............$14.95

34 CHARLIE BROWN CHRISTMAS
00311228 P/V/G..............$15.95

35. ELVIS PRESLEY HITS
00311230 P/V/G..............$14.95

36. ELVIS PRESLEY GREATS
00311231 P/V/G..............$14.95

37. CONTEMPORARY CHRISTIAN
00311232 P/V/G..............$14.95

38. DUKE ELLINGTON STANDARDS
00311233 P/V/G..............$14.95

39. DUKE ELLINGTON CLASSICS
00311234 P/V/G..............$14.95

40. SHOWTUNES
00311237 P/V/G..............$14.95

41. RODGERS & HAMMERSTEIN
00311238 P/V/G..............$14.95

42. IRVING BERLIN
00311239 P/V/G..............$14.95

43. JEROME KERN
00311240 P/V/G..............$14.95

**44. FRANK SINATRA –
POPULAR HITS**
00311277 P/V/G..............$14.95

**45. FRANK SINATRA –
MOST REQUESTED SONGS**
00311278 P/V/G..............$14.95

46. WICKED
00311317 P/V/G..............$15.99

47. RENT
00311319 P/V/G..............$14.95

48. CHRISTMAS CAROLS
00311332 P/V/G..............$14.95

49. HOLIDAY HITS
00311333 P/V/G..............$15.99

50. DISNEY CLASSICS
00311417 P/V/G..............$14.95

51. HIGH SCHOOL MUSICAL
00311421 P/V/G..............$19.95

52. ANDREW LLOYD WEBBER CLASSICS
00311422 P/V/G..............$14.95

53. GREASE
00311450 P/V/G..............$14.95

54. BROADWAY FAVORITES
00311451 P/V/G..............$14.95

55. THE 1940S
00311453 P/V/G..............$14.95

FOR MORE INFORMATION,
SEE YOUR LOCAL MUSIC DEALER,
OR WRITE TO:

HAL•LEONARD®
CORPORATION
7777 W. BLUEMOUND RD. P.O. BOX 13819
MILWAUKEE, WISCONSIN 53213

Visit Hal Leonard Online at
www.halleonard.com

Prices, contents and availability
subject to change without notice.

PEANUTS © United Feature Syndicate, Inc.
Disney characters and artwork © Disney Enterprises, Inc.